Very Special Birthdays

by Jessica Quilty
illustrated by Nicole Wong

PEARSON

Scott Foresman

Editorial Offices: Glenview, Illinois • Parsippany, New Jersey • New York, New York
Sales Offices: Needham, Massachusetts • Duluth, Georgia • Glenview, Illinois
Coppell, Texas • Ontario, California • Mesa, Arizona

Every effort has been made to secure permission and provide appropriate credit for photographic material. The publisher deeply regrets any omission and pledges to correct errors called to its attention in subsequent editions.

Unless otherwise acknowledged, all photographs are the property of Scott Foresman, a division of Pearson Education.

Photo locators denoted as follows: Top (T), Center (C), Bottom (B), Left (L), Right (R), Background (Bkgd)

Illustrations by Nicole Wong

ISBN: 0-328-13313-2

7 8 9 10 V010 14 13 12 11 10 09 08

Birthdays Are Special

How do you celebrate your birthday? Do you have a party and blow out candles on a cake? Do you get cards and presents from your family and friends?

People celebrate birthdays in different ways all over the world. Some Chinese people celebrate their birthdays with special traditions.

Celebrating a New Baby

Chinese people celebrate a new baby. Family and friends bring special presents. They may bring the baby's family gifts of food.

They may also bring clothing and toys decorated with tigers. Many people from China believe the tigers protect the baby.

The parents have a Red Egg party when a new baby is one month old. Aunts, uncles, cousins, neighbors, and friends all come to the party.

The parents tell everybody the new baby's name. The parents also give red colored eggs to each guest. Red means happiness. The eggs mean new life.

The baby's mother collects presents from friends and family. Some guests give the baby food. Grandparents may give the baby jewelry made of silver or gold.

Other guests may give the baby money wrapped in red paper. Red paper means a good future. The parents may save the money in a bank for when the baby grows up. At night there is a big dinner for all the guests.

First Birthday

Another special tradition happens when the baby is one year old. The mother or father holds the baby. The family gives the baby a basket filled with different objects and toys.

There may be a doll, a truck, a spoon, or a pen. Everyone watches to see which object the baby touches first. The family believes that the object the baby picks shows what his or her future job will be. Which object do you think you would have picked?

Birthdays for Children

Sometimes, birthdays are celebrated with a lunch of special noodles. These noodles are very long. The long, unbroken noodles represent a long and happy life.

Family and friends may be invited to share the lunch for the birthday celebration. They wish the child a long life. Guests may still bring gifts of money wrapped in re

Turning Sixty

A Chinese person's sixtieth birthday is very important. Everybody shares eggs, noodles, and candied peaches. Peaches are another sign of long life.

The Chinese one-month and sixtieth birthdays are the most important. What part of these special birthday celebrations would be your favorite?